"*Blue If Only I Could Tell You* is a book of journeys and arrivals, of the many far and consequential places we might find ourselves: Punjab, Tipperary, the sandy banks of the Platte River in Nebraska. Exquisitely plainspoken, clear-eyed and wise, Tillinghast is keenly aware of the histories and stories that shape our worlds; these poems roam and wonder and find homes for us everywhere. 'You gave me a compass,' the poet writes, 'and here it is / on my table / pointing north.'"
—Joe Wilkins

"These are troubadour poems, wandering back in time and far in space, finding their tunes in a Southern childhood of farmland and fishing, in India, the American West, Hawaii, and Ireland, alert to 'ghostings/ of rain' and to the astonishment of 'apples falling through the Milky Way.' Tillinghast's cadences feel deeply, richly, surprisingly true to life. And abundant in the heart's intelligence."
—Rosanna Warren

"Richard Tillinghast's new collection of poetry is the book we need right now, assuring us that music can be heard in the silence and dread will always, eventually, give way to hope. His poetry is infused with dark humor and casual wonder. Lyrical, conversational, clear-eyed and mystical, the poems in *Blue If Only I Could Tell You* are the kind we'll return to again and again. This is a book that has been inspired by the present, informed by the past, and is sending a love note, while sounding a warning, to the future."
—Laura Kasischke

BLUE IF ONLY
I COULD TELL YOU

poems

Richard Tillinghast

White Pine Press / Buffalo, New York

White Pine Press
P.O. Box 236
Buffalo, NY 14201
www.whitepine.org

Acknowledgments appear on page 105.

Publication of this book was supported by a grant from the National Endowment for the Arts, which believes that a great nation deserves great art; by public funds from the New York State Council on the Arts, with the support of Governor Kathy Hochul and the New York State Legislature, a State Agency; and with funds from The Amazon Literary Partnership.

Printed and bound in the United States of America.

Book design: Elaine LaMattina

ISBN 978-1-945680-51-9

Library of Congress Control Number: 2021941545

This book is for Suzy

Contents

3

4

5

Exodus

Homage to Muriel Rukeyser

The refugees were nervous,
  glancing back toward the hills,
fearing the sniper with his telescopic sight
        and sinister nickname.

    What did these homeless ones care
about the history of human displacement?
  They were changing money
    and trying to sell their watches.

Trucks packed with soldiers—
  boys really—sped along the dock,
    firing their rifles into the air.
I think the gypsies were the most afraid.

Then came a truck with a loudspeaker
  moving slow among incinerated cars
on the boulevard named after the national hero,
    giving orders in three languages.

How many souls, how many dreams of escape,
      how many nightmare nights
            could the little ship hold?
They took on board as many as could pay.

Small groups gathered on deck talking quietly.
    It was an end and a beginning.
Someone had brought a bottle
            and they needed it.

What a sigh ascended when the ship steamed out
        onto the uncaring ocean.

A Way Station in the Punjab

A scattering of impromptu lean-tos
      under trees among grasslands.
A well and a pump for washing,
a camp kitchen where soup bubbled,
   an open-air prayer space swept at dawn,
sprinkled throughout the day to keep the dust down.

They gave me a place to roll out my bedding,
     read and make sense of my travels.
The stars and planets burned through blackness
an astonishment pure diamond,
       apple-green and scarlet.
I dreamed of apples dropping through the Milky Way.

I was a young man then, without complications—
    before the wars of religion, before
  the towers burned. Borders were open,
travelers found a welcome, people were kind.
      Then history swerved
     and the world reverted to chaos.

Refuge

A little house above the tsunami line,
plumbed, wired, and swept.
Tatami mats on the floor.

Trade winds riffling the palm fronds.
A place to heal. And the knowledge
there is work to be done.

Doves' throaty calls, saffron flashes
of finches, and the rice birds
that hang upside-down on stalks and peck at seeds.

Starbucks, or a train compartment,
or a room at the airport hotel
outside Mexico City, it's all very well.

But this is better. You've brewed me a tonic.
You've painted the door red and the walls green.
The orchids are in bloom.

You gave me a compass, and here it is
on my table,
pointing north.

I

One thing I did not foresee . . .
the growing murderousness of the world.

—W.B. Yeats, *The Trembling of the Veil*

The Boar

for Laura Kasischke

That bristly motherfucker.
I'd run out and yell at him
when he came onto our land—
him and the sow and the seven piglets.
I threw rocks
and made a big noise.
But he was not inclined to flee.

As I made a move toward him
trying to look menacing,
he set his trotters into the ground
and feinted back,
more sudden than me.
I could see him thinking, "Come on, take me on
if you've got the balls for it,
tall two-legged animal
with whatever that is you're wearing on your head.
See these tusks?"

So Barry the pig guy came, set his snares
on the pig-trail through the *hau* trees
and trapped him.
"What the fuck!" the boar bellowed,
"I have absolute right here!
"I forbid this!"

Barry lassoed the pig and bound him
hind legs and front,
dragged him squealing out of the thicket.
That fellow would go to the pit.

But the cry that boar let loose
as he struggled against the ropes
split the peaceful sky of our hilltop.

The chickens ran under the house,
dogs barked in houses half a mile away.
And God knows what the baby goats next door
made of it.
Nobody had instructed them yet
about borders and killing and rage.

The Allies

I'm going down there again tonight
      to call on the allies.
To touch, insubstantially,
my forehead to theirs,
to breathe the breath they breathe,
      and ask them for strength.

Used to be, at twilight, they would spring up
      in the corners of my eyes.
It could scare a person.

Now they choose invisibility
and embed themselves under stones
      within earshot of
handclaps and temple drum-pulse
and water sounds
      from the pool
where they purified themselves,
      overgrown with weeds now.

The earth has absorbed them,
the grass reclaims their laughter,
their sweat.
But not their dominion.

I'm going down there again tonight.

Driving to Meet You

Rain all day. Nutmeg waxbills
      rise in flocks from the sugarcane.
The road is running with overflow.
          My heart brightens.

From shore, runway lights fairy-tale in the bay.
      Shadows transit
along the margins of the cane fields—
      piglets and sows out foraging.

My truck bumps down the rocky track toward town.
      Horses standing in fields of rain,
fragrance of guava trees along the way.
      I see the lights of your plane coming in.

Boat

A door in the afternoon opened,
 the barometer fell a notch,
 the day turned inside out.

Out over the ocean I saw ghostings
 of rain, a granular
shimmer of drizzle coming ashore.

Big drops saucered on the banana leaves.
And when I hoisted an umbrella and walked
 out into it, the rain
said something to the umbrella I raised.

It was the opposite of big shouldered or insistent,
 but steel
wouldn't have stood a chance against it.

And who was I
 in the midst of it all?
"The highest good is like water,"
 Lao Tsu wrote.
"Water gives life to the ten thousand things
 and does not strive."

I wanted to be a leaf buoyed up by the current
 on a river a child imagines
while he plays in the gutter in a rainstorm.

It's raining in the story too,
 and they're out in a boat,
 the boy and his dog.

The White Egrets

for Steve Pearlman

Who lives up there
    I wonder—on the ridge beyond us
        over the gulch
            where the stream
speaks syllables in the night
    when I go to my window and listen.

No business of mine,
    but I catch, at times, voices.
The wind blows toward me
    the laughter of children,
        a cry of rapture,
voices raised in anger on a difficult morning.

What connects
    these lives of ours lived at a distance,
bridged by the air that separates and joins us?

White egrets
    flapping home to nests in the sea cliffs
by threes, by sevens, by twelves,
    view from their altitude
        our valleys and misty hillsides.

A feather floats down from what they know of us.

At the Edge

As he feeds his chickens, cooks rice,
    sweeps out his shack,
  he hears the droning of enemy planes.

Dreaming of temples and waterfalls
         he wakes to
the thwack-thwack-thwack of helicopter blades.

    Comes the thud of a mortar,
the man fills a thermos, latches the door of his shack,
and creeps up the slope in moon-dark,
      his dog sticking close.

    Up near the top of the ridge
his dog makes a low sound in her throat,
  smelling before he does, diesel,
    the unwashed bodies of soldiers,
      the stink of hastily dug latrines.

His dog sneezes, and he clamps his hand
      over her nose.

I can evade them, he thinks.
    I can survive out here,
I know how to hide.

But what of the town-dwellers?
What of the scholars,
  whose knowledge they want to erase,
    whose books they will burn?

What of the women
    who live alone on farms?

The clanking of tank treads,
the rising dust of an army on the move.
Dawn must be
            closer than he has
allowed himself to understand.

Four Horsemen

St. John of Patmos is hammering away
     about four horsemen:
It's all there in the Book of Revelations.
I've tacked up the Dürer print of those riders
on cardboard the size of a movie poster.
It blocks out the sun in my sunny room.

Christos has lived and, some say, died.
  The Romans are worried.
The Mediterranean buzzes with
     visions and sightings,
mobs roaming with hammer and nails
  and lengths of hardwood.
A betrayal kiss, thirty pieces of silver,
  a stone rolled away from a tomb.

And now here John is—
     raving, so the islanders say—
John the Revelator,
  renegade from the seven churches of Asia,
an outlier the peasants give wide berth to,
living on spring water and
     bread he bakes on flat rocks
        in the blinding sun of his island.

Four horsemen like outlaws in a Western—
     archer king on a white charger,
swordsman on a red warhorse,
black rider with a full head of curls.
        And scariest of all,
Behold a pale horse, John writes,
and his name that sat upon him was Death.

One Raindrop

Brando's hand, unsuspecting,
              cradles an orange at a sidewalk stall
on location in New York in the forties—

              the sky darkening

I get up from my big-screen TV
        and scan with field glasses
                          the hard wind driving
              from seas north of the island
                    rattling palm fronds, shredding.

Moods being weather,
        who argues with a storm like this?
        Unless you're out on the moor, a king,
                    pelted by rain.

And then there was the storm
        the night they tried to assassinate Michael
in *Godfather II*—
        the curtains undrawn, Diane Keaton asleep
in their bed, an uptick of wind, thunder,
                          waves choppy on Lake Tahoe.
And then the machineguns.

But nothing like the storm unloading now
        around our blue-marble orb.
The Pacific swirls with garbage,
        plastics choking the frigate bird,
the monk seal and albatross, the green sea-turtle.

Trade winds slap slack canvas,
        sea-gyres stall off the beaches and cities
              of North America.

Gulf Stream weakening in the Atlantic,
          warm waters lapping
up city streets along the Jersey shore,
the Monsoon Current in the Indian Ocean
                bristling with tsunamis.

2

the true sound of history, this metal against bone.

—Jim Harrison

The Blind Singer of Swannanoa

Blind,
        but her fingers on the fretboard
find paths through the dark.

I follow her voice
    along creek banks
        into the hills above Swannanoa

where the lost nation
                wintered in bluffside caves,
            lit campfires they hoped the white men
                        wouldn't catch wind of,
    and carved their thoughts into limestone.

Wild canaries take up her song,
whippoorwills serving out the term of their bondage
                night by night,
and the mockingbirds mocking them.

Folks around here
                believe troubled souls
visit burying grounds despite prayers
    laid down by preachers over open graves,
    and they call to each other in the voices of owls.

Who knows what presences
   rise from these hills
         to hear her song—
the fire builders and basket weavers
         who were hunted down and shot.
Runaways an hour ahead of the bloodhounds
         and slave patrols.
Deserters who stripped the insignia
         from their sleeves
and limped wounded into the backwoods to die.
The stragglers and bushwhackers
         who knew what it is to kill a man.
The pretty girl who went for a walk with her lover
         and was never seen again.

Play their song for me.
         I want to live in that darkness.

At a Campsite Outside Ogallala, Nebraska

The air expands greenly,
      snaked with lightnings
            and the pounding of thunder.
Wind lifts the native grasses,
    long hair flicked like wheat over a white girl's shoulders.

And a freight train's diesel horn, horizontal, crazy,
      the shut-shut-thud of rail cars over the track
          toward Omaha and Chicago
   from docks in Portland and San Francisco,

        sky buffeted by summer's beginnings.

    Camped out along the sandy, willowed Platte,
what did those old Lakotas make of these onslaughts,
      these heaven-animating epiphanies
        back when the plains were theirs entirely?

    Storms rake across the interstate.
Inside my tent I spread out across a camp table
        maps of my journey.

      Semis veer off for havens under
cottonwoods blown silver-dollary in the sky's fierce horizontals.

What is this, hail?
      It clobbers my tent roof, and the low-slung
    double-wides and two-rooms over on the reservation.

It must have caught them, too, back then, from time to time
           as they traveled,
the Hunkpapas, the Brulé, the Miniconjous even,

though they kept to themselves along the riverbeds
and didn't like to be intruded upon.
The Two-Kettles, who feasted on antelope,
Santee, Ogalala—whom people called
"those who camp apart from the others"

and the Sans Arcs, the "without bows"
who fire, all the same,
arrows into the storm clouds tonight.

Thousands march toward the Bighorn Mountains,
Blackfeet, Cheyenne.
Around them their pony herds,
camp dogs yapping about the rain,
their women and children, their captives,
white as well as from other tribes, miserable, beaten-up, bruised,
their holy men and singers,
their old and sick on lodgepole travois.

The man they call Thašúnke Witzó, Crazy Horse,
paints white hail
spots on his body—I see him—,
streaks a lightning bolt
red down one side of his face
with buffalo blood.

Behind his ear he ties a brown pebble—
sets on his head a hat made from the
feathers of a red-shouldered hawk.

He passes through the storm untouched.

Living Near Horses

      I would wake in the night
hearing horses breathe in the neighboring field,

      horses I neither owned nor rode.

One of the little herd would whinny
                       and once
            like Lakota ponies
   two horses galloped,
        their hooves struck hard dirt
              in the moonlight.

They knew we were here, we knew they
                  were there. Mine
      was the paint.

But one day she was taken from me,
      put in a trailer and driven away.

  She was not young.
     it was only when I was giving her
an apple once, I noticed how chewed down
         her teeth were.

      She was my friend, at times I felt
   she was my darling.
         I was not a man
    who wanted to tame her,
fasten tack on her.
     We met over the fence.

I remember how at first she would look at me
     with flight and terror in those wide-apart eyes.

I would stand at the fence, an apple in the
                                pocket of my jacket, and
                                        talk to her.

In time she would amble over,
            pausing to crop the coarse grass in her path.

I liked how her jaw felt under my hand
                                as she chewed
                    and rubbed her nose against my chest,
            her jaw molded smooth like the jaw of some

            long-ago marble horse
                                in a museum,
        brought into the traffic and alarms of the city
                        from a parthenon on a hill.

    I liked walking back to my shack
                        with the smell of horse on my shirt.

Mimbreño

A chunk of mesquite
sizzled against the bricks of the old man's fireplace,
and popped. That's what you get,
he thought, and it woke him.

His tooled leather saddle lay on the floor,
and his Apache saddle blanket.
He had grown old, and made his peace. He reached
for the silver cup he drank mescal from.

He had fallen asleep on the horsehair sofa,
saw himself in the beveled glass
mirror across the room.
That's what you get, the old Mimbreño mumbled,
and then knew he was talking to no one.

The wounded were delirious, he remembered,
begging for water,
the strips of rawhide
he gave them to chew on for the pain ·
turning bloody from their head wounds.

The soldiers had Sharps rifles,
.52 caliber.
They could fire from hundreds of yards
away, and the wounds were grievous.
The men were cut to pieces—
limbs, brains, chunks of bone.

If they brought up the cannons he knew
he would be singing his death song
before sundown,
and he heard the weird, minor-key
intervals of it in his head.
"Now the change comes over me," he sang.
He had killed that day,
and his heart was glad.
Then the canyon rang with the deep voice
of artillery above the rancheria.

But then why was he alive now, why was he
old, drinking mescal from a silver cup?
Whose life was this?
A black thunderwall rolled up from the southwest
over the mesas of Old Mexico. The wounded were begging
for a drop of water.
The cup he drank from, of hammered Mexican
silver, stood on the marble-topped table a few
inches from his hand.
Whose life was he remembering?
The violence of the storm

came of a sudden.
Sheets of it blinded the men
as they lay in the wallow facing outward,
firing their carbines and muskets.
The storm blotted out the encircling troopers.
Rivulets of rainwater
pooled where they lay.
Muddy as it was, and bloody too
as rain ran down from their clotted wounds,
they lay down on their bellies and drank.

Weave

It's not just a basket
      though woven, plaited, pleached.
In the clutter and dust on my table,
      among my pens and ink,
it's an object of power.

I work my fingers around the sphere of it,
      feeling it give and push back.
  It's not much bigger than a walnut.

      Maybe what I like best,
its fiber creaks when I grip and unflex.
        That's its voice.

The man I bought it from braided it from honeysuckle,
    which must be why
when I hold it to my nostrils and draw a breath
      I'm in a canebrake by a river,
         leaves turning, the air rich.

Picture a creased roadmap, the basket maker driving west
from Tahlequah down 62 out of the Cherokee Nation,
    station wagon filled with baskets.

It's a light load. Empty and fragrant it rides.
  He picks up the interstate at Checolah
and follows it through Oklahoma and the panhandle,
    past the stockyards at Amarillo,
      sleeping in the car at a truck stop.

He makes New Mexico next morning,
      breakfast at McDonalds,
on his way to the Indian market in Santa Fe.

On top and bottom he fashioned
a seven-pointed interlocking knot,
        then wove a globe around that
from thirty-three or thirty-four
            circular windings.

A sphere? You could say so—
        yet it's asymmetrical, a leaking moon
            full of stories.
There's woodsmoke in there,
  a scorch of deer meat roasting.

But what's this?
        Hold it to my ear and I hear rifle shots,
a horse alarmed, one man shouting to another in English,

someone running down a creek bed
    bleeding, feet
  freezing, lungs tight to bursting.

    And then the weave of it
unclenches, and it's there on my table again,
  beside a strange pen and a bottle of ink.

Smoke

My schoolteacher friend drove me
  in his schoolteacher's-salary Subaru
from the lighthouse in St. James, explaining.
    I liked riding in the wet-wool fustiness
of that car, with its car-heater warmth
          and up-north funk.

I liked jamming my boots down into
    the days-old crumpled-up
fast food wrappers and old newspapers,
      and I cleared with my glove
circles in the frost on the windshield
        as we bumped off the blacktop.

Then there we were on foot in the mud and rain,
circumnavigating the circle of stones—
        I counted thirty-nine—leaving offerings
    where others had left theirs—coins
and trinkets: a St. Christopher, a couple of jacks,
  a lipstick, a rabbit's foot, a dime-store ring.

Someone a thousand years ago
  chiseled into one of the stones
what looked like a rune. The weather
      had not erased it. My friend said
on the solstice the rays of the rising sun
  lined up across the circle's axis.

And that was when the car full of Anishinaabe
appeared—Ojibwe from the look of them—,
      their car even older than ours.
I watched as they took tobacco from a pouch,
      lit it and lifted up some words
                into the smoke and drizzle.

Did that smoke, did those words
    keep their circle unbroken
in the life they lived among us in this America?—
        invisible most days, their lives unchronicled
in the newspapers crushed underfoot
    inside the schoolteacher's car.

A Photograph from the Indian Wars

for Andrew Tillinghast

They shadow me, these trees
    from a century and a half ago
on a postcard I bought in Montana.

Something has been lashed to their branches.
    You can just make it out through the sepia.
They're burial trees, those bundles are bodies.

I know these trees, or ones like them—
    black cottonwood, green ash, box elder.
After a long day I pitch my tent and camp in their shade
            on my pilgrimage west.

They gentled their wounded,
        the Lakota and Cheyenne,
                    on sledges made from saplings
as they trekked south toward the
        White Rain Mountains,
            pausing only to bury their dead.

They washed the blood from the dead men's hair,
    dressed them in what finery they owned,
lashed them to branches with strips of buffalo hide,
    and pointed their feet toward the rising sun

so that the dead might not lie in mud and water,
        the chant went,
    so that wolves might not dig up their bodies,
so that animals might not walk over their graves.

Contagion

Trappers who stumbled onto
a Blackfoot village in 1840
saw tipis standing smokeless. Smallpox.
*Wolves ran about the village, fat
and impudent. The Indian dead
hung in swarms in the trees
and buzzards
sat in rows along the bluff, gorged
with human flesh, drunk on ptomaines.*

Fargo at night, 2020,
a man stands in the parking lot of Fargo General
looking up at a window in the Covid ward
where a woman lies face down, intubated.
Coyotes trot unbothered
through downtown streets.
Lights burn at night in the coffin factory,
saws whining.

3

Crossing a river, crossing a county line, crossing a state line—
especially crossing the line you couldn't see but knew was there,
between the South and the North—
you could draw a breath and feel the difference.

—Eudora Welty, *One Writer's Beginnings*

Highway 61

for Susan Williford Montgomery

Night dropping over the big river.
Smoke, and a freight-train whistle
        blowing in from Arkansas
as we ghost down South Third
          and off the exit ramp

onto the two-lane ribboning south,

      our talk in the car hushed
by the voices of insects,
         rows of cotton plants
running to the horizon
  where the massacred wilderness stands—

creeks filled with the memories of dead men,
     shagbark hickories, sweetgums,
        an oak tree
with a rope swinging from a limb,
     and the ghosts of old mahoganies
           watching us.

Jungling scuppernong vines
    hang in the branches
up there with the witness of wild canaries.

A dog barks as we unlock a gate,
      our headlights illuminating
  the glistening skins of magnolias.
A mastiff on a chain
   licks our hands in welcome
      at the door of the cypress-battened
farmhouse, its acres moonlit around it.

We'll sleep here tonight.
What dreams will arise
        to trouble our repose?

Two Scenes from a War

for Marlin Barton

I. Stones River, New Year's Day

Sixteen thousand men
bivouacked deep in rebel country
bedrolled between the sunken rows of corn.
At first light they begin to stir,
trying to start cookfires
with rails they've broken off farmers' fences
with their rifle butts.

This is a war to set men free.
That's what the preachers told them
back in Massachusetts and Ohio.
Whether they think about that
as they pace back and forth trying to get warm,
hawking and spitting, lighting their pipes,
shitting in shallow field-latrines,
history does not record.

A rabbit bounds out of the forest,
then more rabbits, and whitetail deer, and a family
of bobcats, coveys of quail—
the beating of their wings louder
than it has any right to be.
In seconds, volley after volley of musket fire
tears them to pieces.
They break and run,
their officers shouting commands,
but that doesn't stop them.

The rebels crash out of the woods—scary men
from the hills. They're skinny, unwashed,
desperate, and they know how to shoot.
It doesn't matter that their boots are worn out,
their general drunk and
falling off his horse, the rebels
keep coming.

Two days later a burial party finds a Union soldier,
his grip stiffened by rigor mortis,
holding the handle of a coffee pot.

2. Breakfield Road, July 3rd

It was a bluebird day on Breakfield Road
and the breeze smelled of blossoms.
The letters on the brass button I had dug up
out of the field read C.S.A.

My bike was leaning against an oak,
and the sunshine warmed me.
I scraped the crusted crud away
with my thumbnail.

A cloud passed over the sun
and I saw the dirt that had smoothly
registered the imprint of my bicycle tires
churned to mud, malodorous

with excrement and blood, the sharpness
of gunpowder burning the horses' nostrils.
Shouting, the officers
running alongside the men.

It had been child's play for the orators,
the silk-waistcoated men
with acres in cotton and sugarcane,
to sell this war to them.

But all that was gone. Their boots
were in shreds. They were sick
of the whole thing. Not an army now,
it was everyone for himself.

I saw the men ripping
the insignia from their sleeves
as they ran, vanishing
into the summer woods.

A House in the Country

In memory of Caro Armstrong

As a child I played at being invisible
to my elders, who had their own lives to live.
Sometimes it seems unreal now, even to me.
They gave me the run of the place, from the kitchen
where hams hung in the rafters darkening
in the rising smoke, and an old woman
sat in a chair by the fire smoking a pipe
and basting venison as it turned on a spit—
to the attic where heat-struck porcelain
dolls stared vacantly, cheeks rouged, limbs missing.

The library was airless and gothic, bindings
crumbling in the wilderness miasma—
Urn Burial with otherworldly illustrations
and *The Flowers of Evil* by Baudelaire
with Aubrey Beardsley's etchings, hardly suitable
reading for a child of my tender years.

Caro kept the accounts and ran the farm.
Penelope's room was tiny. It was where
she painted her miniatures and brooded.
Linley and Trooper kept an office in town
where they played at practicing law.
I wonder if they had any clients at all.

I wandered the fields and woods with my .22
under scuppernong vines trailing from old cypresses.
Wild canaries sang up there in the forest roof
and cottonmouth moccasins swam in the creeks.
Nobody ever told me to be careful.

Around the dinner table with its *outré*
talk and wideness of permission, an itinerant
artist had painted Italian country scenes
with Roman ruins that somehow entered
the conversation without being mentioned.
Isolation, dipsomania, who knows
what else. The wreck on the highway, the Packard
gone over the bridge into the river that night.

The evangelists who visited on their rounds,
after accepting the house's hospitality,
eating their fill at that blasphemous merry table
and sleeping warm, shook the dust from their feet
before they moved on, as advised by Scripture.

Two Graveyards

Square columns carpentered by slaves
rose above my head.
Leaves swamped the veranda
where dirt-daubers built their laddered homes
and a wren scolded as I peered into
rooms furnished with dust and brokenness.
Up the staircase I guessed
there were bedchambers where a family's lineage
had been engendered,
where children were nursed through illness,
eyelids closed with silver coins.

At the end of a boxwood lane I found the family plot,
stones enclosed within an iron fence.
Next to an obelisk and a Celtic cross
an angel grieved.
Names not used anymore, born-and-dieds,
far countries and near counties, a motto in Latin,
were chiseled into marble.
I traced with my fingertips
letters eroded by rain and frost.

Where the red clay sloped away
a second gathering of stones surprised me—
none larger than a loaf of bread.
No words memorialized
what remained of
hands that chopped and ploughed,
lifted and carried, wrung the necks
of chickens, and rocked the cradle
up there in that house where paper roses
peeled from the walls.

Law Enforcement

The moon was so bright that night, so luminous
when I left the party, and I was feeling so fine,
what with the whiskey and the smoke going round.
I could have walked home, it was no great distance.

But I drove. The mockingbirds blew lyrical,
late-night jazz played on the radio, fireflies
illuminated freshly mowed lawns.
I switched off the headlights, slipped into neutral

and glided down the long slope past the baseball
diamond and the Equestrian Center.
I was making maybe two miles an hour tops
in the Lexus, the gradient was so gradual.

It was only after I had made the turn
onto Canterbury Way that I noticed
the squad car behind me—no siren, no flashing
lights. This was one very patient policeman.

I coasted down my driveway, shut off the engine
and rolled the window down. "Just wanted to
make sure you got home safe, sir," the young cop said.
I was a homeowner, white, a taxpayer in our little town.

There was no breathalyzer, no license check,
no flashlight in my eyes, no straight line to walk.
I was doing nothing dangerous
like going for a burger, or driving while Black.

Cake

The city she lived in was not
   the city I lived in, even though we lived in
      the same city.
In my city people didn't carry a gun
   in the glove box of their car as she did.

I never learned Ollie's last name,
and now there's no one left alive
     who could tell me.
   She watched over me most days,
while Mama taught French at the girls' school.

There's no going back in time
    but I wish I could go back.
       I'd like to get inside
the mind of this woman
     who was paid to look after me.

The music she liked, I liked.
  The station she listened to, I listened to.
One of her eyes looked straight and one looked sideways.
  She'd been kicked by a mule, she said,
and maybe I believe that and maybe I don't.

She was partial to country music
—which was thought odd— so we listened to
   honkytonk angel songs while she ironed
    and stood at the stove
 making her hot water corncakes.

After Ollie moved back down to the country,
the cake she baked every year on my birthday
    didn't travel well. She would put it in a pasteboard box,
        and mail it to Memphis.
Every year I opened a box of crumbs from her.

A Flutter of Fabric

A flutter of fabric, a breath,
  something stirring

in the branches of a tree
  overhanging a graveyard—

a graveyard on a grassy hillside.
Nobody goes there anymore.

But there's this hymn or something
        I keep hearing.

And if I am singing—
singing to a dearly beloved—
does she live in a place now
        beyond all that we know,

   beyond earshot,
beyond heartbeat and ardent glance?

Something not living
        lives in the music tonight.

Dispersal

A city block,
          most of its houses demolished.
Now a parking lot, office block,
convenience store,
brick duplex where all were
                    white clapboard with gabled roofs.

                    An impulse comes searching,
sits in a parked car and has a smoke,
          rolls down a window to look
at porches where rocking chairs creaked,
                    invisible now—
                    iced tea with mint from the garden,
fireflies on summer evenings.

          A dismantled library. . .
Someone's *Wuthering Heights* from college
                    its cover distressed,
          turns up on a $1 table somewhere.

A man in Seattle makes coffee and settles down
          in front of a rainy window
  with the *Decline and Fall,*
                    pages impressed with the imprint
                              of another's thoughts.

Chipped around the rim and inexpertly glued,
          a delft platter on an estate-sale table
  was part of a dinner service,
                    saw the lighting of candles—

Nothing, surely,
　　　　　to the fragmentation of an empire,
　　　the dissolution of provinces,
small countries with
　　　　　　parliaments and currencies of their own now,
　　　the mother tongue devolving into patois and creole.

A little girl looks out from a picture frame—
　　　sterling, from 1910 maybe.
Someone has tied a bow in her hair,
　　　and they've sat her in this impressive chair.
She smiles, but she's unhappy
　　　now she's someplace no one can see her,
　　　　　　no one who would have known her as a child.

This daughter, mother, aunt, cousin, ancestor—
　　　　　　she's a waif now.

Trotline

I lay bone-light athwart the cross-struts
                in the bottom of the boat
          watching the moon transit

                    while I sipped whiskey,
buoyant as a leaf, under a bankside willow.

I had set a trotline on the South Fork River,

                    secured a line to an oak
then rowed across, bucking the current,
                    and lashed it on the nether bank
to the post of a straggling cattle-fence.

Then tied off half-a-dozen droppers
          and baited treble hooks.

The daytime-green river ran black as moon-dark
          from springs in Missouri

                    and thrummed the six baited hooks
I had cinched to the mainline with Boy Scout knots.

          A dog barked from a distant farm,
an owl worked the stubble field behind me
          for mice that kindled in his infrared.

Catfish awoke, I knew, from the murk on the bottom—
          smallmouth bass and rough-fish rose,
                    drum and gar,
          as day-heat evanesced off the river.

The moon dropped toward Texas
    and stars frosted the sky's sway of blackness

one night during my life on earth.

Tell Me a Story

Very well.

The heat was like a big hand
        smoothing out the landscape.

Beyond the farmhouse and kitchen garden
    chickens scratched
in the dust of the barnyard.
Pigs sought out the coolness of mud,
                and a cow path
    lazed toward a pond
            green with duckweed.

When the wind dropped
  you could hear a barely audible
        buzz from the bee tree
            where the drive curved.

Smoke rose from the cooks' cabin before day
        and work began at six.
The men had to be fed.
        Then there was the sound
            of a mule's complaints,
a lug-wheeled tractor cranking,
        the rusty creak of wagon wheels

and they were off
        to cotton fields in the bottom land.

2.

But tell me—is it true
          that where there is labor
    there will also be daydreamers
          and those whose task it is to remember?

In his playroom up under the eaves
  of that old hipped-roof house,
    the farmer's little grandson
        spun his idle fantasies
and Grandmother pondered begettings and begats
    in the broad-leafed book
          open in her lap.

The son who went into a far country
        and wasted his substance with riotous living
and collapsed drunk every night among pigs,
              returned one day,
        dragging blistered feet
          through the dust of the road home.

Where Mary and Martha kept house,
an upper room was swept and dusted
        and a bed made up
for a guest both human and divine.

There were born-and-dieds
   in different hands and inks
in the Bible that Grandmother held,
         descending to the present
   in counter-motion to the sky blue
morning glories strung up on the porch
         turning their faces skyward.

The little boy in his playroom
conjured the future from childish imaginings,
like Joseph in exile in Egypt
         who could riddle out dreams—
like the boy, the chosen one,
         the boy who came into the temple
and struck the elders dumb with amazement.

Keeping Company

It was New Year's morning.
Daddy and my brother were watching
        the Rose Bowl parade roll past
on that tiny black-and-white TV of ours.

Mama was cooking the blackeyed peas
  as she did every year.
I had scrubbed the ham hocks
        and sliced the vidalias.

She always said the blackeyed peas
would bring us good luck for the rest of the year.
  "Will it really, Mama?" I wondered aloud.

"Well I don't know, honey,
but let's keep company with the rest of the world
        and say it does."

I was also wondering about the collard greens
   that were supposed to bring money,
      which she budgeted severely
in the leather account book she kept in her desk.

I had made my New Year's resolutions
        that day I'm talking about,
and burned my faults the night before in the fireplace
after writing them on slips of paper Mama gave us,
keeping company with the rest of my now
            faultless family.

Years later, yes,
I keep company with the rest of the world.
I sing the song everybody sings.
I say it's all good. I preach to the choir.
I say it is what it is.

Does it do any good?
Does any of it ever do any good?

Ambrosia

A feast day at Queen Elizabeth's court
        could not have rivaled
            Thanksgiving at the farm.

The men of the family walked the land with shotguns,
        wing-shooting quail the dogs flushed,
then brought their appetites and a whiff of gunpowder
        back with them to the farmhouse

where the turkey awaited, with smokehouse ham
        sliced thin enough to see through.
The aunts' pride of pies deployed on the tablecloth
            like wedding presents on display—
            crusts crenelated, a spicery
of cloves and cinnamon, sugar and tartness.

With the pies there was ambrosia.
Say the word and it opens
    like an ambulatory, a cathedral aisle.
            Then it swerves.

They sliced and sugared oranges in the kitchen,
        then they needed a boy with a hammer
            and a glint of purpose in his eyes
            to deal with the coconut.

And once I had smashed it open and picked up the pieces
        out of the flower beds
            and washed my hands and
the shell was pared off,
                the coconut chopped up and mixed in,

it tasted like rain on the roof on a summer night.
The oranges were the rain, the coconut
the sound the rain makes.

To Find the Farm

It couldn't have disappeared off the map
because it was never on
the map.

A half-forgotten sense of direction led me there
past the Baptist church and the country store,
through woods and across the L&N tracks.

But the farm had been erased.
Chicken house, corncrib, milking stalls,
barn cats, John Deere tractor,

a rat terrier named Pal.
A shed full of tools, a plough,
mules that brayed and balked.

I couldn't take it in. I stood and looked
for the assemblage of labor, the continuum
of seed and soil, weather and muscle,

the intelligence it takes to grow things
that lived here
through bondage, invading armies, hard times.

A farmer and his wife,
half-a-dozen tenants in unpainted shacks.
Cotton picked, ginned, and sold.

Revival

Abandoned on what had been a road,
    a pickup truck,
blue paint purpled by sun,
       and a Model-A Ford

    stalled on this shoulder of the mountain,
sumac growing up through the horsehair seats,
  rusty seed pods in league
       with the rust of the machine.

Creeper interlaces the tines of an antique
      harvester in a field,

     a cooking pot overturned in the yard.

Inside the house, pictures still hang on the walls,
  though they took their Bible with them.
I don't hear the hymns they sang, do you?
     And what has become of their church?

But let this homeplace speak. Let it tell its story

now that the machinery of the world
     starts to misfire,
  stall out, and begin its slow deceleration.

Maybe it's time to disappear
down into the creek bed, quick as we can,
     ahead of what's coming over the mountain

and follow the deer tracks
        and the strange cries of wild turkeys.
Flakes of obsidian, arrowheads, rusty bolts,
            a cannon ball from an old battle,
        bleed into the stream
                that obliterates our tracks.

Could we ride bareback again,
    plow the earth, hunt and trap,
            sew and mend,
    rig a snare to catch the feral pigs,
        build a tabernacle
in the loneliness of the unpeopled mountains?

4

Continent, city, country, society:
the choice is never wide and never free;
And here, or there . . . No. Should we have stayed at home,
wherever that may be?"

—Elizabeth Bishop, "Questions of Travel"

I Tuned Up Seán's Guitar

for Thomas Lynch

I tuned up Seán's guitar
     and gave it an airing
on the flagged forecourt outside Lynch's house,
the wind whipping off the North Atlantic
               three fields from where
  Clare drops into the sea.

Soon I had it ringing
       with songs of my own country,
green mountains, bottomless rivers, deep valleys
    dark as a dungeon and damp as the dew.

I shot a man in Reno, I sang,
      just to watch him die.
              I had no fiddle to liven it.

The foal's whiteness was something not of this world.
Not till tomorrow would she feel
     on her coat, that was new as anything,
  what we call rain.
Camilla licked the foal's leaf-like ears
as I sang out those dire things
  that happened ten years ago on a cold dark night.

Even the black crow left off cawing
     when he heard about the long black veil and the
night wind that moans
        and the living who weep over gravestones.
What business had I
     singing into those still-damp ears
ballads of horseback journeys and murder,
   duels and scaffolds
       from a country she had never heard of?

It was some comfort to know
we shared no common tongue.

My Eye Found It

       from the train,
a big square plot of green
            on a green hillside

no different, seemingly, from the field
       that encompassed it.
Trees had been planted
      to establish a perimeter,
and two stone pillars marked
  some sort of entrance.
But there was no gate I could see,
      no in and no out.

It was as though someone had pegged out
  this right-angled plot of hillside
      as an exercise in geometry
whose purpose I could not fathom—

      a monument to emptiness,
a site where something might at one time have stood
      or might yet be built.

  A cube of space projected skyward.

Diamond

A girl's own heirloom
         cached in a drawer
with the snapshot of a horse, some nail polish
         and a postcard from Venice.
The ring is a source of envy,
         and she loves that.

And even if it's stolen,
            even if the thief
      wraps it in a cloak of deceit and
sleight-of-hands through customs
      and it's sold on the street in Aleppo,
            still nothing dims it.

What is as light, as empty of content
            as a diamond?
Not even snowfall—
            big, clean, absolving.

A Length of Ribbon

He was a fresh-minted penny,
    a riff repeated, a flower in a buttonhole,
    a man who always knew what to say.
A pond you could see to the bottom of.
And though a heron came at the darkling hour
      with a warning in its beak,
he awoke every morning with a smile.

She was a row of blackcurrant bushes
   severely cut back, a radio switched off
    so that one might hear the silence.
She was a derelict farmhouse rebuilt
     to her own exacting specifications,
an impossible task necessitated by an arduous dream,
a flowering cherry tree espaliered to a barracks wall.

I picture them sitting together holding hands
   as the light goes out of the day,
     singing some old ballad
till the twilight takes up their song.
   Once or twice comes a glimpse
of an augury awakening in the underbrush,
  but they don't see it—

these figures whispering on the turret stairs
   in a tower derelict and wind-bothered
as a stripe of lightning splits the sky.
  Though the ink has dried on their story
and their sorrows are wrapped in a length of ribbon,
   I take it down off the shelf on occasion
and summon them reanimated and fervent.

A Sighting in Tipperary

I picture us on one of our rambles
walking up the path to see the old church—
roofless to heaven, apostolic yet pagan,
whatever glass may have animated its windows
gone centuries ago, the tawny sandstone
chiseled crudely but not without art,
chinked with accidents of limestone, some the gray
of the distant sea, some porphyry, some smoky blue
made softer by the softness of the day—
a farmhouse in the distance, a field being ploughed.

Then comes the rain in earnest, and we hoist
our umbrellas to blunt it—and this is when
Dennis appears, so now we are three.
It's the man himself, no one else like him,
unmistakable in that tweed jacket he wore
year in, year out, the leather elbow patches
cushioning his bony elbows, the sparse beard
a shade greyer, but quick as he ever was,
with the high-strung alertness he had when living.
We struggle to mask our astonishment.

He shies from our umbrella, the rain doesn't
touch him, it's unclear he even notices.
As a boy he cycled these roads
with a book and an apple in his pocket.
He could have explained the round-arched door
with its deep-chiseled design, the human heads
sculpted from limestone, unbaptised and angular—
if the dead were allowed the privilege of speech.

And then a procession appears out of nowhere
coming straight at us as they round the gable end,
mourners all dressed in black, huddled against
the downpour, black umbrellas glistening—
all about them the solemnity, the fragrance
even, of ground dug deep and prayed over.

It's all of a piece—these mourners black as crows
among the graves, a priest in an overcoat.
He speaks to Dennis in the island tongue.
Where has he been off to? the old man asks.
Dennis smiles, hesitates, but doesn't answer.
Perhaps this is what he has needed—to feel
the ground beneath his feet again, supposing
he can feel it. A bell tolls, the rain slackens.
And then, like a rainbow that fades, he's gone.

Took My Diamond to the Pawnshop

Neuron pathways overgrown
with brambles and vegetative junk,
meanderings and dead ends,
    forgetting and remembering.

I'm wading through muck,
    scraping silt off
antiquities that bob to the surface.

Let's hose this down and
                    see what sparkles.

A map of the Pacific
                    walks by on a man's t-shirt.
A pear falls.
    The wind blows away my pages.

I followed my dream
and ended up sleeping on the floor,
    thousands of pesos in debt.
Three in the morning and I've never been so cold.

How many times can you land on your feet
    before your feet get sore?

Mezzogiorno

*for Alan Williamson
and Jeanne Foster*

Full summer.
The umbrella pines show burnt umber underneath,
and cicadas scratch out a dry music.

The bells in the valley churches suspend unmoved,
their tongues hanging out.

Paving stones underfoot on the terrace
blossom salmon-pink, copper-tarnish, verdigris.

Every color goes with every other color,
even the faded football jersey
of the man out taking a stroll.

Children's voices from a hedged garden levitate
and—there!—a white shuttlecock
half-moons over the arrow cypresses.

But who's this
out for an airing?
A butterfly,
heraldic and unheralded,

as if these two wings
and they only
had kept themselves under wraps
while everywhere under the sun
spring edged into summer,

and now they find their moment to appear—
buttercup yellow and bold as a banner.

Overnight

It *is* gloomy,
especially in the rain,
the waterways with mist rising off them,
memories of past visits
and earlier loves—
ghost smudges barely glimpsed,
dripping alleyways,
steps dissolving into water,
old ladies behind curtains
eating off trays,
lives that have themselves become riddles.

Then it changes overnight.
The salt breezes open one's nostrils to delight,
the tourists are suddenly not
so dowdy and badly dressed.
The canals glitter that famous jade green,
the *motoscafi* fly their tricolor pennants bravely,
and the sky is once again
that cerulean blue the painters loved.

Persian Journey

The country people could hardly
   fail to notice our caravan,
        the fineness of our mounts,
our leopard with her jeweled collar.
      And flying in advance of us
          our falcons,
   their eyes incandescent.

When we drink with these rustics
  in their smoky tavernas
     they comment on
our robes' silver stitching, the polish of our tack.
      And seeing I am a man of learning,
  they ask me about the star.

Is it always necessary—
          I think but do not say—
for the eyes of men
     to penetrate the ways of the most high?

I lie openly
when they ask me
    why we are traveling.
  I talk about spices,
    I talk about incense.
    I talk about precious metals.

5

The bee emerging
from deep within the peony
departs reluctantly.

—Basho

Blackbird

The ascent,
dark as skin on a moonless night.

A hawk
      bumps across the landscape
under benighted hollies

carrying and killing
in his talons
      a blackbird.

There were days
I would mount this precipice with joy,
      pilgrim staff in hand.
The candling chestnut tree—
      an icon, a lighthouse—
stood rooted on the summit
      as a guide.

No longer the seeker I was,
  now I walk the via media.

But what are these
      harmonies I hear
now that the sky darkens

and the blackbird's
cry becomes my own?

Shade

So fine, to stretch out
      in the shade of a cottonwood
on a splayed and spring-busted old couch like this one,
and pluck the strings of a guitar
             while the slow river purls.

Now and then a trout rises
        and the roar of the four-lane
whispers over these copper-colored hills.

And wasn't it in the cool of the day
      when Jahweh himself
        was walking in the garden
holding the book he was reading
      open behind his lordly back?

The Book of Love, let's call it.
    He was always eager to learn.

When he found them out
      he might have pulled one of his really nasty
        Old Testament stunts.
But he stayed his almighty hand.
Things could have been worse for them
        and for us.

Far worse.
"Without strife," wrote Hesiod,
"there is no greatness."
Even if strife means sunlight splintering
      outside the Gates of Eden,
        the bruised heel, the dust of migration,
  sweat pouring off your face—

wailing, it is true,
     she holding ashamed hands
         over her apple breasts.
He—while a snake slithers away through the undergrowth—
        gives out such a cry,
     speaking the first poem up toward the concealed stars,

as to be heard in the four corners
                   of the newly formed earth.

Early Church

Silence inside the cold edifice,
                              household of the word,
                  sailing ship of the spirit.

A winding path leads up to a door—
                  red-berried holly, clipped yew,
            granite slabs standing upright,
                              names mossy, dates neglected.

The stonecutter's hand, the woodcarver's
                        chisel and mallet
            cut crockets and quatrefoils,
legends of martyrdom, a saintly rabbi nailed to a cross.

    Everything we believe or don't believe or half-believe
or once believed, or aren't quite sure about
                  floats in this enclosed air.

A jar is broached, an amphora of scented oil.
            A woman laves
                  with Aramaic hands
feet dusty from Galilean roads,
                  —the words of her story echoing in
the language of gnostics and empire builders.

But she doesn't hear any of this.
She kisses the man's feet, her tears falling for all time,
                  drying them with her hair.

And so with a whiff of scent,
                  a whish of seersucker,
                        we open our little books and kneel.

Leavetaking

Of course it was raining
when I stepped outside
        on the little porch,
naked except for a towel.

Greenness lit up the morning.
        Redwing blackbirds
piped in the rushes at the lakeshore.

  Outside, the car awaited,
my belongings inexpertly packed.

Other cars move in my direction,
domestic creatures only.

Rain pings on the windshield,

        the moment of indecision
folded like a handkerchief
        in my back pocket.

What I Learned, and Who I Learned It From

Stephen Sandy taught me how to drive in snow—
"the art of the approximate"
as we fished-tailed,
drinking beer,
over the roads around Bennington.

I learned from Bob Cogswell
how to gap sparkplugs
and how to adjust the valves on my little Volkswagen
lying on my back underneath the car
in summer, or when it was really cold,
on concrete or gravel
in my garage in Berkeley
or under cottonwoods in Arizona.

And when the clutch cable snapped
I found I had learned enough
to make it from Grass Valley to Mill Valley
without a clutch,
starting it with a jerk in first,
easing off the accelerator in accordance with the Tao,
slipping it into second breathlessly,
and finally into fourth
for that long drive through the night.
I guess I learned that from John Muir's book.

From the book my grandmother
would hold in her lap and read
and doze off, I learned
that a soft answer turneth away wrath,
that in our Father's house are many mansions,
and that the lilies of the field toil not,
neither do they spin,

and yet they outclass King Solomon
any day of the week.

My mother taught me
to always carry a clean handkerchief,
how to pick out a good lemon,
the names of half-a-dozen constellations,
fifty or so trees,
an astonishing number of wildflowers,
and how to break up an old flowerpot
when you plant a rosebush,
and put the shards
in the bottom of the hole you dig.

One or two other things I worked out on my own,
but just now
I can't remember what they were.

Sendoff

What is the water talking about
as I wade out into the current with my fly rod
                    to begin another season?

        The stream-rubbed coinlike
                        pebbles it will place on my eyelids?
Or the sendoff
                if I'm bundled like Beowulf onto the sea,
my treasures heaped around me amidships,
                    or swaddled in wicker like Moses and
pushed out through bullrushes into the current
where my body becomes flotsam and jetsam, food for fishes,

        gone like the men I fished with—
the drinkers and tellers of tales
and the rest of our brotherhood,
                    the madmen who cast into
        moon-shadowed pools
                    at three in the morning—

            all of us
    lost in the mist,
            barking at shadows,
                    keeping ourselves company.

How Old Was I?

Glimpses of something hidden under layers,
                a cache uncovered
            from where?

        From the cinders of Pompeii
written on the Roman equivalent of Wm. Morris notepaper?

Scroll or papyrus shall we say, beeswax seal,
            the Roman version of a canceled stamp somewhere,
me as the recipient, a Roman boy
                with one of those funny Roman haircuts.

How old was I?
                Seventeen maybe?

After I had read it five or six or a dozen times
        I hid the note.
    Maybe I didn't want Mater to find it.

So I hid the letter under a stack of books
                (only we didn't
    have books back then, but never mind).

And that's where it stayed, I guess,
            for centuries—hell, for decades,
years, days even!

under the lava.

But maybe I've got the time period wrong.
            Maybe that letter
        was postmarked in this century, or the 20th.
                Or maybe I'm lying.

The note was in French no doubt, or Latin
or else in English. Or Italian,
        the language of volcanoes, arias, canals.
    And it told how one loved with all one's heart
        and yet something stood in the way.

Or . . . Or maybe a way could be found!

    It was all there in that letter,
that document in the history of the heart,
of that thing that happens to you
        that's like wolves—

        the pages of the letter
vellum, or William Morris notepaper
    or parchment or papyrus—noble somehow,

self-assured,
    curling at the edges in the flames from the eruption,
            scorched, disappearing.

Almost Home

I feel a twinge of it,
a darkening in the western sky.
A bell sounds,
open and empty
over standing pines.

The ocean, a journey,
leaving my belongings behind.

They await their handling
in the care of those
whose property they now become,
their placement in other rooms.

An owl's syrinx flutters,
a peregrine shifts in the trees.

The ocean, a journey.

Blue If Only I Could Tell You

Homage to García Lorca

I.

Blue if only I could tell you
       how much I love you blue.
When I buy ink it's you I go looking for.
Even before the sky turns blue and
  I get out of bed and pull on my Levis
I sail my gaze out
      over turquoise and ultramarine,
salt breeze and leagues of ocean.

2.

Not *Officer, he beat me up* blue,
not *His fingernails are turning blue.*
   I fill my pen with königsblau,
     listening to Miles and
vanishing into the inkwell's unfathomable O.
     I sniff the breeze for direction,
minding the tilt of swells and the tide's mood swings.

3.

Shakespeare, in that movie they made about him,
  his fingers, whenever the camera let you
     see his hands,
         were blue with ink,
even when he shimmied up
the rich girl's father's palace wall.
This was the hand that wrote
     The lights burn blue, it is now
  dead midnight.

4.

Do you remember your first set of oils?
Cobalt like Hokusai's *Great Wave of Kanagawa*
or the underside of a Winslow Homer swell
           in a storm off Barbados,
the sharks beside themselves with anticipation,
                 rolling like dogs.
Aquamarine like a summer morning in Laguna.
  And the tube of navy like World War II,
victory at sea taking off from steel-gray carriers
and men in blue pinstripes
           who made their fortunes off munitions.

5.

Is it hard sometimes to know just who you are?
Green shimmers to the east of you, purple to the west.
           From the lapis of your earrings
    comes the resonance of temple bells.
In the sapphires on your bracelets I hear
           the blue whales singing
      as they launch up from the depths.

Richard Tillinghast was born and raised in Memphis. After college at Sewanee he did graduate work at Harvard, where he studied with Robert Lowell. The author of thirteen books of poetry and five of creative nonfiction, he has received grants from the Guggenheim Foundation and the National Endowment for the Arts, the British Council and the Irish Arts Council, and has held the Amy Lowell Traveling Poetry Fellowship. He has taught at Harvard, Berkeley, the College Program at San Quentin Prison, and the University of Michigan in the U.S., as well as at Trinity College Dublin and the Poets' House in Ireland. His poems have appeared in *The New Yorker, The Atlantic, Paris Review, The Yale Review, American Poetry Review, The Best American Poetry, The Best of Irish Poetry,* and elsewhere. His book reviews have appeared in *The New York Times, The Wall Street Journal, The Washington Post, The New Criterion,* and other periodicals. He has been awarded the James Dickey Prize for poetry from *Five Points* and the Cleanth Brooks Award for nonfiction from *The Southern Review.* His 2000 book, *Six Mile Mountain,* was reprinted in 2021 by StoryLine/RedHen. Currently a member of the Core Faculty in the Converse College MFA program, he is Emeritus Professor of English at the University of Michigan and a founder and past Director of the Bear River Writers' Conference in Northern Michigan.

Tillinghast has long been a student of Turkish culture, having first visited Istanbul in 1964 as Editor of *Let's Go,* the student travel guide, and returning there many times since, often with the support of grants from the American Research Institute in Turkey. In 2009, in collaboration with his daughter, Julia Clare Tillinghast, he published *Dirty August,* translations of the 20th-century Turkish poet, Edip Cansever. His literary travel guide, *Istanbul: City of Forgetting and Remembering,* was published in London in 2012 and translated into Turkish a year later. He has also had a long association with Ireland, living in Galway for a year in the early 1990s and in Tipperary from 2005 to 2010. For many years he wrote for *The Irish Times* and other Irish periodicals. Salmon Poetry published his *Today in the Café Trieste* in 1997, and Dedalus brought out his *Selected Poems* in 2009 with an introduction by Dennis O'Driscoll. The University of Notre Dame Press published his *Finding Ireland: A Poet's Explorations of Irish Literature and Culture,* in 2008. Richard's 2017 book, *Journeys into the Mind of the World: A Book of Places,* University of Tennessee Press, recounts some of his other travels. He currently lives in Hawaii and spends his summers in Sewanee, Tennessee.

Acknowledgments

Grateful acknowledgment is made to the editors of the following journals where these poems have appeared or are scheduled to appear:

AGNI: "Early Church"
The American Journal of Poetry: "The Boar," "A flutter of fabric," & "Or"
The American Poetry Review: "How Old Was I?"
The Asheville Poetry Review: "Contagion" & "Refuge"
Bear River Review: "At a Campsite Outside Ogallala, Nebraska," "I Tuned Up Sean's Guitar," "My Eye Found It," & "Shade"
Birmingham Poetry Review: "Trotline" & "What I Learned, and Who I Learned It From"
The Café Review: "Diamond," Refuge" & "Dispersal"
Catamaran: "Boat"
DMQ Review: "Sendoff" & "Took My Diamond to the Pawnshop"
Delmarva Review: "At the Edge," "Canzona di Ringraziamento," "Daddy's Hands," "Law Enforcement," "One Raindrop," & "The White Egrets"
Gavialidae: "Ambrosia" & "Highway 61"
Great River Review: "Revival" & "Smoke"
The Hopkins Review: "Blackbird" & "A Sighting in Tipperary"
The Hudson Review: "Cake," "Leavetaking," "My Eye Found It," "A Photograph from the Indian Wars," & "Tell Me a Story"
Image Journal: "Persian Journey"
Michigan Quarterly Review: "At a Campsite Outside Ogallala, Nebraska" & "Two Graveyards"
The New Criterion: "A House in the Country," "A Length of Ribbon," "Mezzogiorno" & "Overnight"
Pine Mountain Sand & Gravel: "Living Near Horses" & "To Find the Farm"
Poetry Ireland Review: "I Tuned Up Seán's Guitar"
Poetry Northwest: "Emblems"

Salmagundi: "The Allies," "The Blind Singer of Swannanoa," &
    "Blue If Only I Could Tell You"
Southern Poetry Review: "Almost Home"
Spillway: "Driving to Meet You"
3rd Wednesday: "I Tuned Up Seán's Guitar," "Keeping Company,"
    "Mimbreño," & "Umami"

"Shade" was included in *The Eloquent Poem: 101 Contemporary Poems and Their Making,* Persea Press, 2019.

"Blue if Only I could Tell You," "The Boar," "I Tuned up Seán's Guitar," "Leavetaking," and "Took My Diamond to the Pawnshop" are included in *Ice Melting on a Hot Stove,*" Clemson University Press, 2021.

Author's Note: As for the sources and genesis of some of these poems: "Exodus" was inspired by a scene from Muriel Rukeyser's prose book, *The Life of Poetry.* "Boat" evolved from a prompt I gave myself based on one of Rosanna Warren's poems from her book, *So Forth.* The quotation in the first stanza of "Contagion" probably comes from Paul Wellman's *Indian Wars of the West,* though I haven't been able to find it again. The account of the battle between the U.S. Army and the Mimbreño Apaches in "Mimbreño" also comes from Wellman's book. It will be clear to readers of Irish poetry that the statement format of "A Length of Ribbon" derives from Michael Hartnett's poem, "The Death of An Irishwoman." "Took My Diamond to the Pawnshop" plays off of Leonard Cohen's song, "That Don't Make It Junk." Much of "Persian Journey" was inspired by Benozzo Gozzoli's paintings in the Medici Chapel of the Palazzo Medici-Riccardi in Florence. Those who know Gozzoli's "Journey of the Magi" paintings will recognize the images.

THE WHITE PINE PRESS POETRY PRIZE